MY TWO OXFORDS

.

Willie Morris
My Two Oxfords

Wood engravings by John DePol
Afterword by JoAnne Prichard Morris
Photograph by David Rae Morris

University Press of Mississippi   Jackson

www.upress.state.ms.us

The University Press of Mississippi is a member
of the Association of American University Presses.

"My Two Oxfords" first appeared in *Homecomings*,
published by University Press of Mississippi in 1989.

Library of Congress Cataloging-in-Publication Data appears on last page
British Library Cataloging-in-Publication Data available

I AM A SINGULAR CREATURE, among the handful who has dwelled for any length of time in two of the world's disparate places—the Oxford in England and the Oxford in Mississippi. On the one hundred fiftieth anniversary of the founding of the Mississippi one, I address myself to the subject. May I suggest there are similarities, but not all that many?

Still, it has always struck me as poignant that the white settlers who first came to this spot in the red hills of northeast Mississippi in the 1820s and 1830s, cleared the piney woods and made churches and roads and schools and jails and had a courthouse square for themselves by the time of the Civil War (everything being in readiness for Federal General A. J. "Whiskey" Smith to burn it all down in 1864), named their town *Oxford*. They wanted to acquire the new state university to dignify their raw terrain, and they were happy they got it, by a one-vote margin of the legislature.

The namesake is rather more venerable. Its first mention was in the Anglo-Saxon chronicle of 912 A.D., and of the university in the twelfth century, although legend ascribes the origins to Alfred the Great. My own Oxford college, New College, was new in 1379, and God knows what might have been transpiring in the forests and swamp bottoms of Lafayette County, Mississippi, in that auspicious year.

Has any single place on earth of comparable size produced such an august and eclectic array of human beings as the English Oxford? Indulge me this casual list, in random order: Thomas Browne, Samuel Johnson, A. E. Housman, William Penn, John Wesley, William Gladstone, Thomas More, John Locke, Lewis Carroll, Philip Sidney, Edward VII, Cardinal Wolsey, Randolph Churchill, Max Beerbohm, Bishop Wilberforce, Matthew Arnold, Robert Peel, T. S. Eliot, Walter Raleigh, Cecil Rhodes, Cecil Day-Lewis, Lord Bryce, Christopher Wren, William Blackstone, Lord Salisbury, Percy Bysshe Shelley, Clement Attlee, Joseph Addison, Richard Steele, Oscar Wilde, Edward Gibbon, John Galsworthy, Charles James Fox, Siegfried Sassoon, Thomas Hobbes, Admiral Blake, Evelyn Waugh, Walter Pater, General Haig, Lawrence of Arabia, Charles Lyell, Lord Baltimore, Cardinal Newman, Arnold Toynbee, Adam Smith, Robert Southey, Algernon Charles Swinburne, Quiller-Couch, Thomas De Quincey, Lord Asquith, Lord Grey of Fallodon, King Olav of Norway, Prince Felix Youssoupoff, who assassinated Rasputin, and General Fridelin von Singer, who commanded the German forces at Monte Cassino. This is a mere sampling, but imagine the oppressiveness of their footfalls as their spirits stalked a callow young American there a generation ago.

I lived almost four years in the classic Oxford in the late 1950s. I came down from New York to the Mississippi Oxford in 1980 to be writer-in-residence at the University of Mississippi and I have been here ever since. Was it the call of the name? Was there something in the blood compelling one to risk assimilating these most dissimilar landscapes? As with other of the curious and divergent experiences of a lifetime, can the two Oxfords be assimilated at all? Or are they both to me a dream?

Certainly that other Oxford is dreamlike to me now in its unfolding, a Lewis Carroll fantasy for a golden summer's afternoon. From the summit of the years I find it difficult to conceive I was actually there. Does this seem strange? Surely it was the first and last time I would ever live in a museum. Its spires and cupolas and quadrangles, its towers and gables and oriels and hieroglyphs, its ancient walls with the shards of glass embedded on top, its chimes and bells resounding in the swirling mists, made home seem distant and unreal. I lived in frigid rooms overlooking a spacious Victorian quadrangle, a stone's throw across the greensward from a massive twelfth century wall with turrets and apertures for arrows. A boys choir sang madrigals every afternoon from the somber chapel across the way. I dined in a gloomy medieval hall with its portraits of parliamentarians and ecclesiastics, warriors and kings. The dons at first were as terrifying to me as nuns in my childhood.

The sacrosanct privacy of the place, the perpetual fogs and rains, elicited a loneliness, an angst and melancholia such as I had never before known. The mementos of death were everywhere, in the ubiquitous graveyards, in the interminable rolls of the war dead in the chapels. The spirit of Kipling and Rupert Brooke resided amidst these scrolls to the fallen young. It was "the City of Dreaming Spires," and "the Home of Lost Causes." The burden

3

of the past was ominous and incontrovertible. The college gates were padlocked at midnight, and within our forbidding fortress we were at the mercy of the ghosts of the centuries, and a squinty-eyed mystic from New Delhi peregrinated in the doomed hours conjuring all of them. After four years at a huge American state university—the final one as editor of the largest student daily in the United States—the change was horrendous. I began spending considerable time in the pubs with the Australians. Emerging from the Turf Tavern one foggy late afternoon into a secret medieval walkway which led to the college, we happened upon a curious assemblage: elves and fairies and Elizabethan princes and princesses and a girl in white robes playing a flute. "I had too bloody much *this* time," the Aussie from Brewarrina, New South Wales, said, unaware that the college drama club had just finished a Shakespearean rehearsal.

Lectures were optional. One of the English students explained to me that they had gone out of vogue with the invention of printing in the fifteenth century. Examinations were comprehensive and came at the end of three years. The tutorial system was the core of the Oxford education. Students wrote weekly or twice-weekly essays and discussed them in private sessions with the dons.

I remember my first essay. The tutor, Herbert Nicholas, had assigned me the Reform Act of 1832. I read seven or eight books and perused a half dozen others. I stayed up all night polishing my effort to a thundering conclusion. Before a gentle fire in the don's rooms above the college gardens I read the next-to-last sentence. "Just how

4

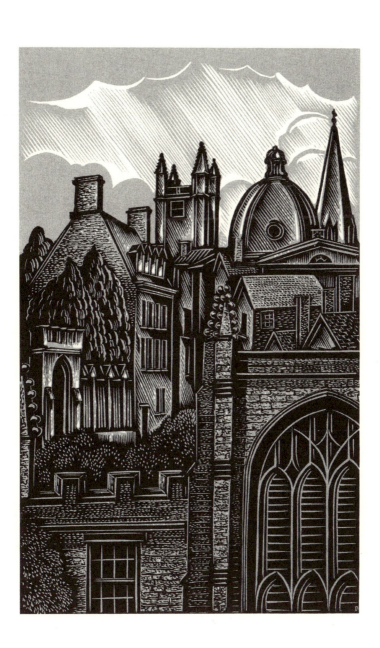

close the people of England came to revolution in 1832 is a question we shall leave with the historians," and was about to move on to the closing statement. "But Morris," interrupted the tutor, "we *are* the historians."

With the essays the only formal requirement, one might do as he pleased: read novels, write poetry, walk along the river, sleep till noon, go to London, bicycle through the Cotswolds, or spend sixteen hours a day reading for the next tutorial. A West Point man claimed he went to the bulletin board near the tower-gateway twice a day looking for an order telling him what to do. The community did not judge, nor interfere with, one's personal habitudes. In fads and eccentricities, as in the paths the mind took, the Oxford student was protected by a subtle yet pervasive tolerance. There was an abiding homage there to independence and self-sufficiency, to intellectual candor, to one's own intensely private inclinations.

The paradox and variety of the place were vivid in its social life. There were social functions right out of Edwardian Oxford—from sherry in a don's rooms on Sunday morning to the raucous society dinners with their several courses and four or five wines. On one such evening W. H. Auden, brandishing a large carafe of red wine, wagered me a one-pound note that he could consume the contents in less than a minute. He did so, then collapsed on the floor. There were the fabulous commemoration balls on the college lawns with the all-night champagne, the tables laden with turkey and goose and pheasant and beef and fish and caviar, and the London society orchestras playing through the dusk-like lingering midsummer nights. At twilight one evening in the college cloisters, the guests, ranging from recent graduates to lords and ladies of the realm, sipped champagne and heard the madrigals sung by the boys choir. There was a time, also, for pork pie and inexpensive sherry at someone's lodgings—the Saturday night parties given by the working-class students where, in one or two close and smoky rooms, dozens of undergraduates were crowded inescapably together. Here invariably was a white wine concoction, American jazz from the gramophone, the shy and awkward English talk between boy and girl.

All this has been hard for me to fit into the whole of my American life, and I am no exception. A number of other American writers, from Robert Penn Warren to Reynolds Price, have studied over the years in Oxford, England, but by and large they have not written very much about it. It was an exotic interlude, and I remember it with affection and love and fulfilment and no little bemusement. Oxford, England, is likewise a commercial and industrial center of well over 100,000 people. Oxford, Mississippi, minus the university students, is an unhurried courthouse-square hamlet of about 11,000, surrounded by a rough and authentic rural countryside. In physical aspect my latter Oxford is closer to the more pastoral Cambridge, without its aura of age or its majestic colleges. Of all the towns and cities in America which are home to the historic, capstone state universities, this Oxford is the third smallest, just behind Orono, Maine, and Vermillion, South Dakota.

Ole Miss is small, too, by measure with other state

universities, with slightly more than 9,000 students who are suffused with the flamboyant élan of their American state university contemporaries everywhere. Indeed, unlike the historic Oxford of my past, I find too *little* loneliness here. The emphasis is on gregariousness. The Greek system is strong and entrenched and dominates the social and political life. The rich sorority girls drive baby-blue Buicks with Reagan-Bush bumper stickers. They are noted for their beauty and their gossipy style. Many of them major in "Fashion Merchandising," an intellectual pursuit absent from the curricula of Oxford, England. Their social life is elaborate, organized, and not especially introspective. A New York writer described the rituals of the sorority rush week: "What screams, what cries, what an amplitude of passion. The proceedings are more exotic than the Romsiwarmnavian rites of the primitive Shirentes of Brazil's rain forest." Yet the legendary beauty of the Ole Miss coed is not myth. The girls of Oxford, England, so stringently screened by some of the world's most demanding academic requirements, were often dour; yet the occasional warm-spirited beauty among them was always worth the waiting, and these were the girls, I am pleased to say, that the Yanks got. By the same token, the intellectual Ole Miss sorority girl of good and gentle disposition is a joyous song in the heart, and will endure.

Surely it would be frivolous and indeed self-defeating to compare the students of one of Western civilization's greatest and most ancient institutions with those of a small, isolated Deep Southern American university.

Yet in moment, there is a palpable, affecting sophistication to this stunningly beautiful campus in the midst of the rolling rural woodlands of the American South. In the juxtaposition of town and school many have been reminded of the Chapel Hill of a generation or so ago, which bustles so now within the perimeters of the Research Triangle. It has so lost its touch with the Carolina land. One often recalls at Ole Miss Thomas Wolfe's description of his only slightly fictional Pulpit Hill years ago in *Look Homeward, Angel*: *"There* was still a good flavor of the wilderness about the place—one felt its remoteness, its isolated charm. It seemed to Eugene like a provincial outpost of great Rome: the wilderness crept up to it like a beast."

Ole Miss ranks high on the list of American Rhodes Scholars, and as with all state universities there will always be its cadre of bright, imaginative, and hardworking young. Gerald Turner, the resourceful new chancellor who is the youngest in the history of the Mississippi Oxford, wishes to build on the sturdier traditions. Turner has succeeded in a $43 million fundraising campaign to improve faculty salaries and the library at the university of the poorest state in the Union, and to strike a more wholesome balance between the Greek and independent students, and to stand fast with the First Amendment.

Nowhere is the contrast between the undergraduate life of the two Oxfords more striking than in two enduring institutions of these different locales: the Junior Common Rooms and the Hoka. The *"J.C.R.'s"* of the colleges of Oxford, England, were the traditional student retreats

9

for relaxation and conversation. These were sedate and proper places with frayed carpets and overstuffed Victorian furniture where one retired for tea and crumpets or to read *The Times* or *The Guardian* or the *TLS*. Women were not allowed (in the English Oxford of my era the colleges were rigorously segregated between the sexes) and the repartee was—shall one suggest?—restrained. In the quiet and civilized gloom one would gaze out the windows at the darkening mists or the incessant rain. I was the only person who read there the *Paris Herald-Trib* for the baseball scores. If time weighed too heavily on my contemporaries and me in this setting, we might retire at pub-time to a little oasis of tranquility called the Turf Tavern—an ancient inn accessible only by a narrow medieval passage and presided over by two old maid sisters and their soporific cats—for warm ale around its stone and timbered bars. Here Thomas Hardy's Jude the Obscure courted Arabella the barmaid, but that was before our day.

The Hoka of the Mississippi Oxford, named after the tenacious Chickasaw princess, is situated across an alleyway from a bar reconverted from an old cotton gin. One is witness in this boondocks avant-garde coffeehouse to the true variety of Ole Miss and Oxford life, as opposed to the enclaves of Sorority and Fraternity Rows. It is presided over by Ron Shapiro, a much beloved St. Louis transplant, a kind of white Jewish Rastaman, and one Jim Dees, a Deltan who writes essays under the nom-de-plume "Dr. Bubba." The auditorium in back will have the classic European and American movies. Up front B. B.

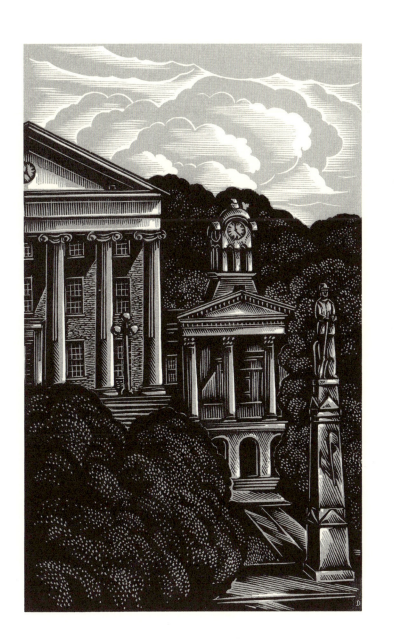

King will be on the stereo, or the Grateful Dead, or Hank Williams, or Elvis. The Memphis and Jackson newspapers are there on the counter, just as the London papers were in the New College J.C.R. So, however, are vintage issues of *Playboy* and *Field and Stream* and the *Yazoo City Herald*, and a wicked journal called *Southeastern Conference Football*. The patrons will include black athletes, willowy sorority beauties, nocturnal professors, a few carpenters or truck drivers or hairdressers from town, tousled student intellectuals in from a lecture by William Styron or Alex Haley or Eudora Welty or C. Vann Woodward, a black and white softball team, attractive female pharmacy students dining on Hoka chef's salad sprinkled with Dixie herbs and seeds, young editors who have just put the student paper to bed, a defrocked fraternity man or two sitting in a corner writing poems, a group of Ole Miss men recently returned from frog-gigging in the Tallahatchie River bottoms who smell of frogs, legal secretaries of both races from the courthouse square, a table of black sorority girls talking football, law students discussing torts and civil liberties, graduate history students arguing the Wilmot Proviso, the writer Barry Hannah between books, and an invariable blend of foreign students trying to make something of the perfervid and eclectic dialogue. One recent evening I joined two black and two white South Africans engaged in heartfelt, almost brotherly talk of their tragic nation.

Two or three of the village dogs will wander in expecting a sampling of the cheese nachos or a nibble from the most popular sandwich of the place, called mysteriously

12

"The Love at First Bite." Instead of tea and crumpets, here there are cinnamon coffee, bagels, and New Orleans–style *beignets*. The mood is mischievous but well-behaved, and some of the soliloquies are lyrical. On the walls are posters and circulars announcing rock concerts in the Delta, or blues festivals in the darkest canebrakes, indigenous sculptures, and photographs of Mississippi's writers. There are portraits, too, of Vietnam veterans by a talented young photographer. In the girls' restroom, I am told, there is graffiti too graphic for the toilets of St. Hilda's College, Oxford, England. Yet, as with the English J.C.R.'s, in its own mode this, too, is an honorable place, where words matter yet.

A casual stroll through the English Oxford of my youth would lead one, of course, to some of the impressive landmarks and monuments of the western world. Many was the afternoon I toured the town and countryside alone, or with a favorite English girl, or with visitors from home, absorbing its fleeting grey auras. The winding High Street or St. Aldate's or the Broad was always crowded with the red double-decked buses, bicycles, and trams, and the sidewalks with the townspeople and the undergraduates in their odd truncated academic gowns.

There were the sudden cul-de-sacs and alleyways, the Broad Walk with its avenue of towering elms, the fragrance and intense greenery of spring along the Isis or Cherwell. The afternoon offered limitless possibilities: the lavish interiors of the college chapels and the serene college gardens, the eerie facade of Mob Quad of Merton dating to the early fourteenth century, the grandeur and sweep of Tom Quad in Christ Church, the Crown Tavern near Carfax frequented by Shakespeare, the Georgian houses along Beaumont Street, the grotesque sixteenth century gargoyles in the Magdalen Cloisters, the Martyr's Memorial in front of Balliol with the statues of the doomed Cranmer, Ridley and Latimer, the regency elegance of St. John's Street, the opulence and isolation of Trinity, the self-proclaimed splendor of Rhodes House, the wonderful private retreat of Blackwell's Book Store where the clerks left you alone as you browsed through Gibbon or Macaulay. One might pause in the Bodleian to look at the first editions of Chaucer or Shakespeare or Milton, or in the Ashmolean for its timeless collections. Or one might tarry in a favorite pub and eavesdrop on discourses about Toynbean cycles, French existentialism, the foreign policy of the United States, or the lastest debate in the House of Commons. How I grew to love these walks of my youth in the noble, heroic old town! And touching everything on this day would be the omniscient, indwelling past.

A similar afternoon's tour of the Mississippi Oxford will be another study in catastrophic contrasts. Foremost are the Faulknerian landmarks. Beginning at the courthouse square with its Confederate soldier facing southward and the benches on the lawn crowded with sunburnt men chewing tobacco, one will follow the shady, settled streets with the antebellum houses hidden in magnolias or crepe myrtles. Their names are Shadow Lawn, Rowan Oak, Memory House. One may stroll by the oldest domicile in town, which was built in 1830. In front of the jail aged white and black men wearing Ole Miss baseball caps sit in haphazard conversation. The Ole Miss students speed by in their cars, their shouts and laughter trailing behind them, and there will be dusty pickups with farmers in khakis from Beat Four. The sorority girls have been in their rooms on campus painting their toenails, when one of them shouts: "Anybody want to go buy some *shoes*?" Everything is a blend of the town and the enveloping, untouched country.

The campus will be only a few blocks down University Avenue. Here the town and the university come together. In the bowers and groves lush with dogwood and forsythia in the spring, white and black students sit together under the trees, or drift languidly toward their classrooms. The old Lyceum is at the crest of the hill, and the library with its inscription: "I believe that man will not merely endure . . . he will prevail." Not far from here is the football stadium, where 40,000 people—four times more than the population of the town—will unquietly congregate on the autumnal afternoons.

The differences between my two Oxfords are even more emphatic in their countrysides. The miniature Oxfordshire country beyond the factories and modest brick homes of the industrial workers is one of manicured landscapes, tiny rivers, stone walls and cottages and comforting greens, ancient parish churches and crumbling graveyards and manor houses at the horizon, perfect vegetable and flower gardens, and pristine village streets with antique shops and tea houses. In any direction from the campus or the courthouse square of the Mississippi

Oxford, a two-mile drive or less, is the rough red earth, hard and unrelenting. Black and white farmers amble along the roads. The dark, snake-infested kudzu vines are everywhere, the landscape dotted with creeks and swamps and abandoned wooden houses, and country dogs bay in the distance. In the fields are scraggly cotton and soybeans, and on the horizon are the violent rains and windstorms of the Deep South. The rural hamlets of Lafayette County consist of a few derelict stores, a catfish restaurant, a church or two, a miniscule U.S. Post Office with firewood more often than not stacked on the front porch, and an untidy graveyard—"the short and simple annals of the poor." In such terrain at the proper seasons, one might sight more than a few of the male students of Ole Miss, hunting in the swamp bottoms with their dogs. This is the closest equivalent in the Mississippi Oxford to following the hounds and will not invite an especially intimate comparison.

On returning from their countrysides to each of the two Oxfords, the vistas from afar will also be dissimilar. The sight of the English Oxford from a distance is one of the most imposing and unforgettable in Europe. The sun breaks through and catches its silhouettes, its spires and walls and cupolas all in filigree, its gaunt and self-contained fortress aspect, and this exists for me in memory now as an apparition. The vista of the Mississippi Oxford from a high, wooded hill is of the campus half-shrouded in its dense vegetation, and of the twin water towers of town, and always the courthouse.

FINALLY, each Oxford, indeed, has been a "home of lost causes." In the English Oxford there were the successive changes of religion, the Civil War in which the university declared for the Stuarts and the town for Parliament, the bloody and immemorial political disputes, the executions and public burnings.

Of the Mississippi Oxford, Gerald Turner speaks of the "extraordinary resilience" Ole Miss has shown in its 140-year history. It too is a place of ghosts. Almost no other American campus envelops death and suffering and blood, and the fire and sword, as Ole Miss does. In the American Civil War it was closed down and became a hospital for both sides. The bloodbath of Shiloh was only eighty miles away. Hundreds of boys of both sides died on the campus, their corpses stacked like cordwood, buried now in unmarked graves in a nearby glade. There is a Confederate statue on the campus also, given to the university by the Faulkners as the one on the courthouse square was. The University Grays, all Ole Miss boys, suffered bitter casualties in that war. One hundred and three of their number were in the first wave of the charge at Gettysburg. Through later poverty and political interference and racial crises the institution somehow survived.

In 1962, John Kennedy dispatched almost 30,000 federalized troops during the riots over the admission of the first black student, James Meredith. As we know all too well, two people were killed and scores injured; it could have been worse. As recently as five years ago, several hundred white students marched on a black fraternity house protesting the abolition of the Confederate flag as a university symbol. In 1982, the university observed the twentieth anniversary of the Meredith confrontation. Interracial audiences gathered for an awards ceremony for distinguished black graduates of Ole Miss and for speeches by blacks and whites. The keynote address was given by Meredith.

Black enrollment at Ole Miss today is just under eight percent, in the American state with the largest black population, thirty-six percent. The black students have sometimes complained that they are left out of the social life of the campus. The Greek system remains completely segregated. The varsity athletic teams are, of course, totally integrated, and the outstanding black athletes are genuine campus heroes. The Ole Miss Rebels football team has the highest ratio of black players in the Southeastern Conference and perhaps the nation—fifty-four percent—and the white-and-black band plays a rendition of "The Battle Hymn of the Republic" and "Dixie" called "From Dixie With Love" at sporting events which would bring tears to the eyes of a Massachusetts abolitionist. The chancellor has pledged to recruit more black students in substantial numbers and to increase black faculty members. One cannot help but note here a new spirit of interracial good will. As Professor David Sansing has written, who would have imagined in those precarious days of 1962 that Ole Miss's most recent Rhodes Scholar would be black, or that the grandson of Mohandas Gandhi would come in 1987 to study race relations in America?

Ultimately, one supposes now, I was only an interloper in the English Oxford. When the moment came, I collected my paraphernalia, mostly books, and returned home again to America. It had been the freest time of my life, and I learned there something of myself–my abilities, faults, convictions, prejudices.

As for the Mississippi Oxford, it lurks forever now in my heart. For it is the heart which shapes my affection for my two Oxfords, and across the years brings them ineluctibly together for me.

AFTERWORD

To read Willie Morris is to enter his world—his life, really—where an astonishing array of experiences, fully lived and intensely felt, merge with a capacious reservoir of knowledge and understanding and a brilliant memory. Willie wrote, as he lived, with everything he had. In his essays and in his nonfiction books, experience is observed through the lens of history—both its sweep and its arcane minutiae—and punctuated by literary illusion, political insight, friendship, love of sports, and humor, all of it grounded in an abiding sense of place and burnished with the seductive elegance of the language. So it is with his essay, "My Two Oxfords," published here to honor Willie's memory on the seventy-fifth anniversary of his birth, November 29, 1934.

Willie wrote hundreds of essays. The personal essay especially appealed to him as an effective way to come to terms with a specific feeling or idea. "A writer has so many things churning around in his head," he once explained, "he has to get them down and make sense of them, for his own sanity." In "My Two Oxfords" Willie ponders the singular circumstance of having lived in and loved "two of the world's disparate places"—Oxford, Mississippi, the home of the University of Mississippi, where he was writer in residence in the 1980s, and Oxford

University in England, where he had studied as a Rhodes Scholar some thirty years earlier. In the English one "the sacrosanct privacy of the place, the perpetual fogs and rains, elicited a loneliness, an angst and melancholia such as I had never known before." In Mississippi's Oxford, where "the rich sorority girls drive baby-blue Buicks with Reagan-Bush bumper stickers," he found "too little loneliness." Revealed in these few words is the essential character of two places and of the man who wrote them, as well.

"My Two Oxfords" has special meaning for me. Willie and I fell in love and courted in Oxford, Mississippi, and we honeymooned in Oxford, England. It all happened because of the book, *Homecomings*, in which this essay appeared for the first time. Published in the fall of 1989, *Homecomings* features six essays by Willie and art by the esteemed painter, William Dunlap. As executor editor of the University Press of Mississippi in Jackson, I acquired and edited *Homecomings*. Willie was living in Oxford, Mississippi, on the edge of the campus of Ole Miss. My professional duties required that I work with him in Oxford.

Willie and I had been friends for more than twenty years, having met in 1967 when his first book, *North Toward Home*, was published and he visited his hometown of Yazoo City, where I was then living. He wrote the introduction to a book about Yazoo, which a mutual friend of ours, Harriet DeCell Kuykedall and I coauthored. He spoke to my high school students on a couple of occasions and even entertained a group of my students who were visiting New York for a literary conference. I attended dinner parties with him when he visited Yazoo City and gave a couple of them myself. But our association was never romantic. So, in the late spring of 1989, as I drove to Oxford to meet with Willie and Bill Dunlap and tie up loose ends of *Homecomings*, my son Graham along for the ride, I had no reason to anticipate anything other than a professional experience. Does anyone ever understand the mysteries of love?

Throughout the fall of that year I spent long, glorious Mississippi football weekends with Willie in his "unhurried courthouse square hamlet" and the surrounding "rough and authentic rural countryside." We would meet a cadre of rowdy Rebel friends in the shadow of the Confederate monument on the Lyceum loop for fried chicken and pre-game spirits and then progress en masse to the south end zone. After the game there was raucous celebrating or raucous commiserating that lasted into the wee hours, often ending with a visit to Willie's "boondocks avant-garde coffeehouse," the Hoka. Together, we celebrated the publication of *Homecomings* at the Governor's Mansion and throughout Mississippi; and in the spring of 1990, at a *Homecomings* event, hosted by Senator Thad Cochran in the storied U.S. Senate Caucus Room in Washington, Willie proposed to me before two thousand people! We were married in September, and Willie moved to Jackson.

When American Airlines asked Willie to write an article for their in-flight magazine, our unrealized hopes for a proper wedding trip began to take shape. They would fly us first class to London and on to Oxford, and Willie would observe contemporary Oxford, England, through the perspective of his earlier memories and write about the visit for *American Way* magazine. And, yes, we would tack on a few extra days for a belated honeymoon. We arrived in Oxford for May Morning, the venerable university's annual spring bacchanalia, which begins at midnight on the eve of May 1 with choirs singing madrigals and continues throughout the night and the following day, with dancing in the streets and boat races on the Thames. Our other days in "the other Oxford" as Willie called it, were less frenzied. How cosmopolitan I felt strolling among "its towers and gables and oriels and hieroglyphs" in the thrall of my new husband! We peered into Willie's old rooms on the New College quadrangle, poked into the quaint Dickensian shops and bookstores, and "retired at pub-time" to his favorite spot, Turf Tavern. Willie was at once awash in the memories of his youth and yet keenly aware of the subtlest nuances of the present. His article, "In a Shifting Interlude," appeared in the *American Way* magazine in September 1991.[1] It is an evocative record of our honeymoon, for better and for worse. For there I am, in Willie's unfailing prose, not the fashionable, worldly traveler of my own imagination, but "incorrigibly American in a yellow rain cap and homely walking shoes"! Such is the plight of the writer's wife.

As Willie's writing thrusts one into his personal world,

1. Reprinted in Willie Morris, *Shifting Interludes: Selected Essays*, ed. Jack Bales (Jackson: University Press of Mississippi, 2000), 127–43.

24

so being a part of that world allows you an opportunity to enter his literary vision. His words about our trip to England were the first I read about occasions that I had experienced right along with him. Perusing the graceful words Willie wrote, his exacting and expressive descriptions, moving reflections, and astute insights—and knowing first hand the research and discipline and care that went into creating them—was for me an extraordinary journey into the arena of Willie's literary talent. Over the next ten years, as I became an increasingly larger part of his writing life, my appreciation of Willie's gifts increased. Even today, no matter how much I know about what he wrote and how he wrote it or how many times I read a particular piece, I am awed by the magic of his words.

I am grateful to the University Press of Mississippi—especially to Director Leila Salisbury and my dear friend, Art Director John Langston—for bringing out this marvelous edition of *My Two Oxfords*. I appreciate, too, the generosity of Neil Shaver of Yellow Barn Press for permission to reprint the original prints from its 1992 limited edition. For those who already know and love Willie's work and for those who are reading it for the first time, this volume is a fitting appreciation and a welcoming introduction.

—JoAnne Prichard Morris

This edition of *My Two Oxfords* was inspired by the limited edition first published by Yellow Barn Press in January 1992. The book was reissued by Blackwell North America later that year in a holiday presentation edition. University Press of Mississippi thanks Neil Shaver of Yellow Barn Press and Jack Walsdorf, formerly of Blackwell North America, Inc., for their enthusiastic support. The press also acknowledges John DePol's exquisite wood engravings, and thanks Neil Shaver for allowing their reproduction in this 2009 edition commemorating Willie Morris's seventy-fifth birthday.

Library of Congress Cataloging-in-Publication Data

Morris, Willie.
   My two Oxfords / Willie Morris ; afterword by JoAnne Prichard Morris ; photograph by David Rae Morris ; wood engravings by John DePol.–[Special ed.; 75th Anniversary ed.].
      p. cm.
   To honor his memory on the seventy-fifth anniversary of his birth (November 29, 1934), My Two Oxfords is a special edition.
      ISBN 978-1-60473-570-3 (cloth : alk. paper) 1. Morris, Willie. 2. University of Mississippi. 3. University of Oxford. I. Morris, David Rae. II. DePol, John, 1913–2004. III. Title.
   PS3563.O8745Z4734 2009
   813'.54–dc22
   [B]   2009040404

26